SPORTS IN ACTION

Fishing

in Action

Hadley Dyer & Bobbie Kalman

Crabtree Publishing Company

www.crabtreebooks.com

Created by Bobbie Kalman

Dedicated by Vanessa Parson-Robbs
To my loving husband Rich: you've stolen my heart—hook, line, and sinker!

Editor-in-Chief
Bobbie Kalman

Writing team
Hadley Dyer
Bobbie Kalman

Substantive editor
Amanda Bishop

Project editor
Robin Johnson

Editors
Molly Aloian
Reagan Miller
Kathryn Smithyman

Design
Margaret Amy Salter
Vanessa Parson-Robbs (cover)

Production coordinator
Heather Fitzpatrick

Photo research
Crystal Foxton

Consultant
Michael Nussman, President and CEO, American Sportfishing Association

Special thanks to
Tanisha Burian, Ken Parson, Vanessa Parson-Robbs, Devin Saumier, Dustin Saumier, Dylan Saumier, Bailee Setikas, Shelbi Setikas, Zach Sikkens, John and Ingrid Sikkens, John Sikkens Jr., Therese Burian, Gloria Nesbitt, Peter's Tackle & Bait, Bob Kennedy and Hackensack Children's Fishing Contest, Diane Rome Peebles and The Florida Fish and Wildlife Conservation Commission, and NOAA–Great Lakes Environmental Research Laboratory

Illustrations
Barbara Bedell: page 14
NOAA, Great Lakes Environmental Research Laboratory: pages 7 (all except bottom left), 31
Vanessa Parson-Robbs: page 19
Diane Rome Peebles: page 7 (bottom left)
Bonna Rouse: pages 13, 17, 22, 25
Margaret Amy Salter: page 8

Photographs
All photographs by Marc Crabtree except:
BigStockPhoto.com: page 24
Photo courtesy of Hackensack Children's Fishing Contest - Bob Kennedy: page 27
iStockphoto.com: page 9 (disgorger), 10 (reel), 11 (fishing line), 12 (hooks), 15 (all except top), 22, 26, 29 (top), 30 (right)
Robin Johnson: page 5
Other images by Adobe Image Library, Digital Stock, and Photodisc: pages 6 (top), 15 (top), 18, 23

Crabtree Publishing Company

www.crabtreebooks.com   1-800-387-7650

Copyright © **2006 CRABTREE PUBLISHING COMPANY**.
All rights reserved. No part of this publication may be reproduced, stored in a retrieval system or be transmitted in any form or by any means, electronic, mechanical, photocopying, recording, or otherwise, without the prior written permission of Crabtree Publishing Company. In Canada: We acknowledge the financial support of the Government of Canada through the Book Publishing Industry Development Program (BPIDP) for our publishing activities.

Cataloging-in-Publication Data
Dyer, Hadley.
   Fishing in action / Hadley Dyer & Bobbie Kalman; photographs by Marc Crabtree.
      p. cm. -- (Sports in action series)
   Includes index.
   ISBN-13: 978-0-7787-0343-3 (rlb)
   ISBN-10: 0-7787-0343-6 (rlb)
   ISBN-13: 978-0-7787-0363-1 (pbk)
   ISBN-10: 0-7787-0363-0 (pbk)
   1. Fishing--Juvenile literature. I. Kalman, Bobbie. II. Crabtree, Marc, ill. III. Title.
IV. Sports in action.
   SH445.D94 2005
   799.1--dc22
                                                                        2005022995
                                                                        LC

Published in the United States
PMB16A
350 Fifth Ave.
Suite 3308
New York, NY
10118

Published in Canada
616 Welland Ave.,
St. Catharines, Ontario,
Canada
L2M 5V6

Published in the United Kingdom
73 Lime Walk
Headington
Oxford
OX3 7AD
United Kingdom

Published in Australia
386 Mt. Alexander Rd.,
Ascot Vale (Melbourne)
VIC 3032

Contents

What is fishing?

Fishing, or trying to catch fish, is both a sport and a hobby. People who fish are called **anglers**. Some anglers catch fish to eat. Others fish for sport. Sport anglers release any fish they catch back into the water.

Take it all in

Fishing is a great way to spend time outdoors and to get some exercise. Fishing isn't as easy as it looks, though. To catch fish, you need special equipment, skills, and plenty of patience! Part of the fun of fishing is enjoying nature while you wait for the fish to bite.

These anglers are heading for their favorite fishing spot. They are ready to catch some fish!

Types of water

Anglers who fish in **fresh water** are called **freshwater anglers**. Fresh water does not contain salt. Ponds, lakes, rivers, creeks, and streams are bodies of fresh water. Anglers who fish in **salt water**, or water that contains salt, are called **saltwater anglers**. Seas and oceans are bodies of salt water. Some bodies of water located near seas, such as **coastal** rivers, also contain salt water.

Fish by fish

It takes years to become an expert angler. With practice, you will become more familiar with your equipment and your skills will improve. The better your skills, the more fish you will catch. **Fishing clubs**, such as the one shown above, are groups of anglers who meet regularly to fish. The clubs provide anglers with a chance to learn from experts, to meet other anglers, and to catch fish!

The fishing hole

To catch fish that are far from shore, you can fish from a boat. Use a boat only when there is an experienced boat operator with you, however.

Some fish live in areas of the water that are dark or shaded, such as under this dock. Anglers often fish from docks.

To catch fish, you need to go where the fish live—in the water. Some anglers fish from land. Others fish from boats. Some even **wade**, or walk into the water! No matter where you fish, you must be careful to avoid falling into or being pulled into the water. For important tips on staying safe in boats and on shore, turn to page 30.

Hangouts and hideaways

Fish live in places where they can find food and are sheltered from the sun. They also live in spots that are protected from **predators**. Predators are animals that hunt and eat other animals. Fish often live under docks and lily pads, among weeds, and near rocks and logs. Fish may also be found below dams and waterfalls, where rivers and streams join together, and at **drop-offs**, or places where shallow water quickly becomes deep water.

Meet the fish

Different **species**, or types, of fish live in different types of water. Some fish, such as sunfish, are found only in fresh water. Other fish, such as snook, live only in salt water. Different species of fish also live in water with different temperatures. Brook trout live in cool streams, whereas bluegills live in warmer streams and lakes. Fish that live at the bottom of bodies of water are known as **bottom dwellers**. Catfish and carp are two fish species that are bottom dwellers.

Most fish found in rivers, such as this largemouth bass, are strong swimmers.

Brown bullheads live in ponds, streams, and lakes.

*Saltwater anglers often fish for spotted seatrout from shores, from boats, from **jetties**, or along coastal rivers.*

Walleyes live in shady spots near the bottom of lakes.

The essentials

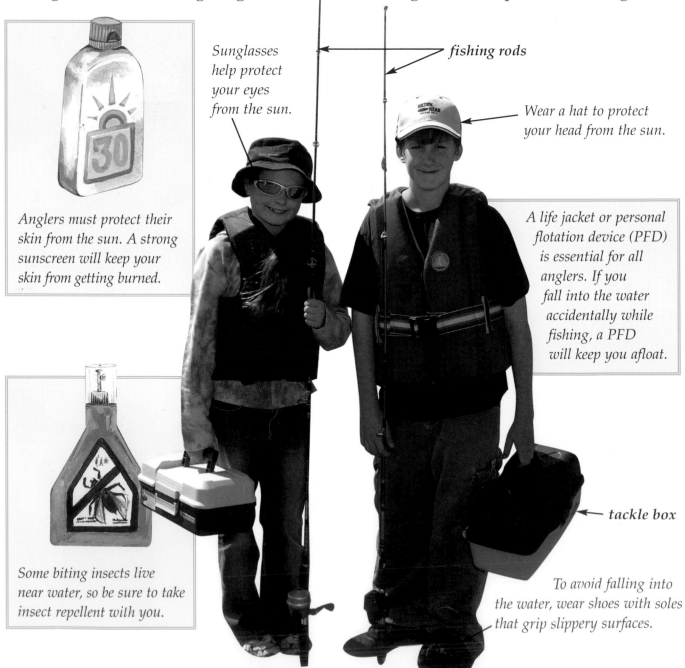

Fishing is a sport that requires a lot of gear. Fortunately, it is fairly inexpensive to put together a basic fishing kit. When fishing, anglers wear layers of clothing that keep them dry and comfortable. Dressing in layers allows you to add or remove clothing if the temperature changes.

Sunglasses help protect your eyes from the sun.

fishing rods

Wear a hat to protect your head from the sun.

Anglers must protect their skin from the sun. A strong sunscreen will keep your skin from getting burned.

A life jacket or personal flotation device (PFD) is essential for all anglers. If you fall into the water accidentally while fishing, a PFD will keep you afloat.

Some biting insects live near water, so be sure to take insect repellent with you.

tackle box

To avoid falling into the water, wear shoes with soles that grip slippery surfaces.

Inside a tackle box

A tackle box holds an angler's **tackle**, or small equipment. Anglers need different types of equipment, depending on which types of fish they are trying to catch.

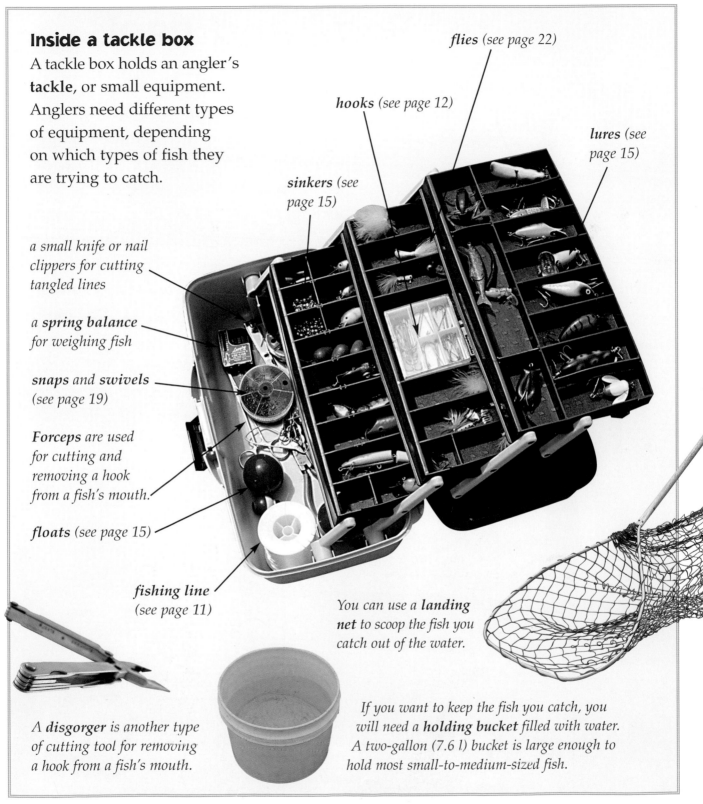

flies (see page 22)

hooks (see page 12)

lures (see page 15)

sinkers (see page 15)

a small knife or nail clippers for cutting tangled lines

*a **spring balance** for weighing fish*

snaps and swivels (see page 19)

Forceps are used for cutting and removing a hook from a fish's mouth.

floats (see page 15)

fishing line (see page 11)

*You can use a **landing net** to scoop the fish you catch out of the water.*

*A **disgorger** is another type of cutting tool for removing a hook from a fish's mouth.*

*If you want to keep the fish you catch, you will need a **holding bucket** filled with water. A two-gallon (7.6 l) bucket is large enough to hold most small-to-medium-sized fish.*

Rods and reels

guide →

rod →

reel →

fishing line →

Every angler needs a rod and a **reel** before he or she can start fishing. A rod is a fishing pole with a handle on one end. Most fishing rods are **flexible**, or able to bend without snapping. A rod's flexibility is also called its **action**. Anglers may use rods that have a little action or a lot of action, depending on the type of fish the anglers wish to catch. **Guides** are rings attached to the rod that hold the fishing line in place along the length of the rod. The reel is a device that attaches to the rod's handle. The reel allows an angler to control the fishing line as he or she **casts**, or throws out the line.

Reel time

Every reel has a handle on its side. By turning the handle, you can wind in the line. Pulling a fish toward you by winding in the line is known as "reeling it in."

Spin-casting

There are many types of rods and reels. This book describes how to fish using a **spin-casting** rod and reel. Spin-casting equipment is a good choice for beginners because it is easy to control. A spin-casting rod has a straight handle and is usually about 5.5 to 6 feet (1.7–1.8 m) long. A spin-casting reel has a cover that prevents the line from getting tangled. You can let out the line by pressing and then releasing a button on the reel with your thumb.

When you shop for a rod, talk to a salesperson about which rods work well for the type of fishing you plan to do. The best rod for you is one that feels comfortable and is easy to use.

Fishing line

Fishing line is strong and lightweight. When you aren't casting it, the line stays wrapped around a **spool** inside the reel. On some reels, a guide called a **bale** keeps the line from getting tangled. Lines are rated by **pound tests** or **tests**. A test is the amount of weight that can pull on a line before the line snaps. Depending on the type of fishing you are doing, you may use a line with a test of only four to six pounds (1.8–2.7 kg). Or, you may need a stronger line with a test of eight to twelve pounds (3.6–5.4 kg).

Fishing line can be purchased on a large spool, as shown above. You must wind the line from the purchased spool onto a spool inside the reel.

Getting hooked

Anglers catch fish using hooks that are tied to the ends of their fishing lines. There are many styles and sizes of hooks. Most hooks have **barbs**, as shown below. A barb keeps a hook from falling out of a fish's mouth. A hook may come already tied to the fishing line on a rod. You can also purchase hooks separately.

Pick a hook

You can buy hooks in different sizes. Each size has a number. Small hooks have larger numbers, and large hooks have smaller numbers. For example, a size-four hook is bigger than a size-eight hook. Small hooks often work better than big hooks do because a fish can take a whole small hook into its mouth. Young anglers should use only small hooks—sizes ten and above.

This young angler is hooked on fishing!

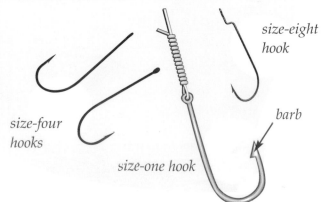

size-eight hook

barb

size-four hooks

size-one hook

Tying the knot

If your fishing line does not come with a hook already attached, you can tie a hook to the line with a sturdy knot. Anglers learn to tie different knots for different styles of fishing. One of the most common knots is the clinch knot, shown below. Other knots include the Palomar knot, the surgeon's loop, and the blood knot.

The clinch knot

The clinch knot is easy to learn. It is made by following these five steps.

1. Insert six to eight inches (15.2–20.3 cm) of line through the **eye**, or hole, of the hook. The part of the line that is threaded through the eye is called the **leader**. The rest of the line is called the **standing part**.

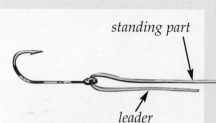

standing part

leader

2. Bring the leader back around the standing part. Wind it around the standing part four or five times.

3. Pull the leader back toward the hook. Thread it through the loop that is closest to the eye of the hook, making a large loop.

4. Insert the leader back through the large loop.

5. Slowly tighten the knot by pulling the hook and the standing part in opposite directions. The loops along the standing part will tighten up near the eye of the hook. Trim the extra line from the leader.

Great bait

Bait is anything that you put on a hook to attract fish. To a fish, bait looks like a meal. The fish can see, smell, or even taste the bait in the water. When a fish tries to eat the bait, you can catch the fish with the hook.

Live bait

Bait that is alive is called **live bait**. Anglers have used earthworms and insects as live bait for many years. Whole small fish, such as the minnows shown left, also make good live bait. Many fish eat other fish, so chunks of fish, shrimp, and clams work well as bait, too.

Baiting the hook

Baiting a hook involves more than tying the bait to the end of your fishing line. If you don't bait your hook carefully, a fish can simply take the bait from the hook or open its mouth and release the bait when you tug on the line. To catch a fish, you must secure the bait to the hook, which will attach to the inside of the fish's mouth.

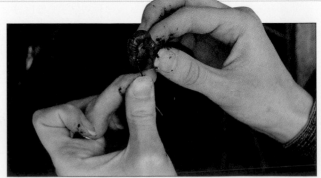

Thread a worm onto the hook to prevent it from being pulled off easily by the fish.

Lures

Instead of live bait, you can use a lure to attract a fish. Lures are designed to catch a fish's attention. Some lures look like worms, minnows, or crayfish. Other lures are simply shiny or colorful. Different types of fish are attracted to different types of lures. For example, many saltwater fish are attracted to shiny metal lures. A variety of lures is shown below.

This trout is about to take the bait. The bright yellow lure has caught its attention.

Lures usually have hooks already attached, so be careful when you handle them!

Floats and sinkers

A float or **bobber** keeps your bait near the surface of the water. A fish pulls down on the float when it takes the bait. Sinkers are the opposite of bobbers. They weigh down the bait and pull it into deeper water.

*Water birds, such as loons and ducks, often eat pebbles to help them digest their food. Sinkers look like pebbles, and the water birds sometimes eat them by mistake. Many sinkers are made of **lead**, which can poison animals. Be sure to choose sinkers made of another material, such as tin, steel, **ceramic**, or heavy plastic.*

Cast away

Learning how to cast is an important part of fishing. A good cast is a sign of a skilled angler. There are many casting techniques, depending on the type of rod and reel you are using and the kind of fish you want to catch. Casting techniques include **underhand**, **sidearm**, and **overhead** casting.

Under, side, or over?

Use the casting technique that feels most comfortable to you and allows you to place your bait where you want it in the water. The underhand technique is useful when you are casting near an obstacle above you, such as a tree limb. A sidearm cast is a fairly easy cast to perform, but you must be careful not to snag a fellow angler! If you are fishing near someone, an overhead cast is the safest cast to use.

Before you head to the water, practice your casting skills on land. Place a target such as a hula hoop on the ground. Stand about 25 feet (7.6 m) away from the target and try to cast your line into it.

Overhead cast

When using a spin-casting rod and reel, the overhead cast is a good method for beginners. Remember, before casting, always check behind you for people, as well as for obstacles such as trees and bushes.

*1. Hold the rod at hip level in your **dominant hand**, or the hand you use to write. The bait should hang from the tip of the rod. Push the casting button with your thumb and hold it down. Position your body so that the target is directly in front of you. Point the rod toward the target, keeping your elbow bent.*

2. Gently raise the rod over your shoulder. Your elbow should remain bent. Continue to press down on the casting button.

*3. Now, lower your arm directly in front of you again. At the same time, lift your thumb to release the casting button and let out the line. When the float lands, turn the reel's handle to bring in the **slack**, or extra line. Hold the rod with the tip pointing up, as shown right. Wait for a fish to notice your bait. If a fish hasn't bitten after a few minutes, reel in your line and cast again.*

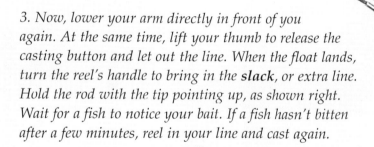

Using the bait

Knowing what to do with your bait once it is in water is an important fishing skill. Bait will work best if you show the fish that it is alive or make the fish believe that it is alive. Fish are more likely to bite your hook if they believe the bait is **prey**.

Luring the fish

To attract fish, make the bait look alive by keeping your rod moving once the bait is in the water. Move the rod in small, slow motions—just enough to make the bait wiggle. When using a **topwater lure**, or a lure that stays on the surface of the water, gently twitch your rod to get the attention of a fish. You'll see and hear a little splash when the fish grabs the lure. Live bait may wiggle enough on its own. Try not to cast too many times using the same live bait, or it may start to slip off the hook.

Bait rules

Many fishing areas have rules that limit the use of live bait. **Undersized fish**, or fish that are not fully grown, may not be used as bait in some places. There may be limits on the number of fish you can catch to use as bait. Some areas have laws against releasing leftover bait fish into any body of water other than the one in which the bait fish were caught. Always learn and obey the bait rules in the areas where you will be fishing.

This angler is using a live minnow as bait.

Bait rigs

A **bait rig** or **lure rig** is made up of all the equipment that goes into the water, including the hook, line, sinker, and bobber. Swivels and snaps are often part of the bait rig, too. A swivel allows the line to turn without getting twisted. A snap allows you to change sinkers, lures, or bait quickly.

Worm bottom rig

sinker   swivel   hook   bait

Bobber and minnow rig

bobber

line

sinker

swivel   snap

hook   bait

Reeling it in

Once you learn how to cast, it is only a matter of time before you'll be reeling in your first fish! Reeling in a fish takes practice and skill. It is important to know the basics of reeling in—if you don't do it properly, you may lose your catch!

Getting a nibble

When you see your float start to move on the surface of the water and feel a tug on your line, a fish is probably nibbling on your bait. Remember, if you try to reel in a fish too quickly, it might get away. Give the fish time to bite into the bait. Point the rod at the float to create a little slack in the line. Then reel in the slack, so the line is tight again. Gently pull up the tip of your rod and give the rod a tug to make sure the fish is caught. If the fish doesn't let go, slowly reel it in. When the fish is close enough to reach, scoop a wet landing net under it while the fish is still under water. Carefully lift the fish out of the water and place it into the holding bucket.

Don't tease a fish once you have caught it. It is cruel to wear out the fish by letting it swim away from you and then reeling it in again and again. Create slack and tighten your line only as many times as it takes to make the catch.

Removing the hook

Removing a hook from a fish's mouth can be difficult and is sometimes dangerous, so it is always best to have help from an adult. First, make sure your hands are wet. Gently smooth back the fish's **dorsal fin** and hold the fin against the fish's body. Hold the fish firmly, but not too tightly. If the hook is in the fish's lip, the barb may be gently eased out of the hole, as shown right. If the hook is deep in the fish's mouth, you may need to use a disgorger or forceps to remove the hook. If the hook is too deep in the fish's mouth to reach, cut the line and let the fish go. Most hooks will **dissolve** over time.

After the catch

If you are going to eat your fish, it is important to have an adult kill the fish quickly to end its suffering. Store the fish in a cooler until you are ready to prepare it for eating. Remember, do not eat any fish that you have caught in **polluted**, or dirty, water.

*Many anglers release the fish they catch to ensure that fish **stocks** stay healthy in their favorite fishing spots.*

Catch-and-release fishing

Once the hook is removed from a fish, you can release the fish back into the water. The practice of letting a fish go is called **catch-and-release fishing**. To increase the fish's chance of survival after you release it, handle it carefully. Reel in the fish as quickly as you can so it does not get worn out. If the fish seems tired, hold it under the surface of the water and gently move it back and forth before you let it go. This movement will help the fish take **oxygen** into its gills. Fish need oxygen to stay alive. You'll know that the fish is ready to swim away when it starts to wiggle in your hands.

Fly fishing

Fly anglers use colorful flies like these to attract fish.

Fly fishing is a method of fishing that uses lures called flies. It is done in fast-moving fresh water such as streams and rivers. Fly fishing is as much an art form as it is a sport. You cast the line back and forth over your head before landing the bait in the water. This method of catching fish is beautiful to watch—and fun to do.

Super-size it

Flyrods are longer than spin-casting rods. Most flyrods are between eight and ten feet (2.4–3 m) long. The long rod helps keep the flyline from hitting the water when you pull your arm back to cast. It also increases the speed of the flyline when you cast. Flyline is thicker than regular fishing line. It is also **tapered**, or thinner at one end.

Fly-fishing gear

To fly fish, you will need light lures called flies. A fly may be made of feathers, fur, or yarn. To a fish, the fly looks like an insect on or in the water. You'll also need a **flyrod**, or fly-fishing rod, and **flyline**, or fly-fishing line. Flyrods are rated by the flyline they are made to cast. Flylines are rated by how much they weigh.

Casting the line

In fly fishing, you will cast your line several times. This technique is called **false casting**. The flyline waving in the air is what makes fly fishing unique. Each time you cast, you'll let out a little more line, until the fly drops where you want it in the water.

Back and forth

There are two steps to casting in fly fishing—the **back cast** and the **forward cast**. The back cast releases the flyline into the air, and the forward cast directs the fly toward the water. When you cast, keep your eyes on the flyline, not on the flyrod or on the fly.

Ice fishing

Even if the weather is cold and there is snow on the ground, it doesn't mean that all anglers must hang up their rods. For ice-fishing anglers, fishing season has just begun! Many fish live under frozen rivers, streams, and lakes in winter. Ice-fishing anglers try to catch the fish that are under the ice.

On thick ice

Before you begin ice fishing, you must make sure the ice is strong enough to support your weight. Ice should be at least four inches (10 cm) thick before you walk on it. As you travel on the ice, you should also watch for open water or holes in the ice and walk only along paths that others have made.

Gearing up

Ice-fishing anglers must dress properly to keep warm in cold weather. Layers of clothing, topped by a wind-breaking nylon jacket, help keep you warm. You should also wear a winter hat, a scarf, mittens, warm socks, and boots.

In addition to winter clothing, ice fishing requires special gear to keep you comfortable in cold temperatures. Fortunately, you can use a sled to carry your equipment across the ice! Be sure to have the equipment shown below when you set out to ice fish.

Ask an adult to use an **ice auger***, or drill, to cut a hole through the ice.*

Use a portable stove or heater for cooking and to keep you warm.

A wooden or plastic ice **shanty** *is a small shelter that protects you from the wind and snow.*

Wearing sunglasses or goggles protects your eyes from the sun and wind.

Use an ice **chisel** *to shape the edges of the hole.*

Warm your body by drinking hot beverages.

Keep your **bearings** *on the ice by checking a compass.*

Sitting on a portable seat will keep you comfortable while you fish.

Use a **skimmer** *to keep the hole clear of ice and slush.*

Fishing derbies

Fishing **derbies**, or competitions, are held all over the world. They give anglers a chance to meet other anglers, to pick up tips, and to learn about new equipment. They also offer anglers a chance to show their skills! Competitors may be divided into age groups for different events. Some competitions are about catching the biggest fish, based on weight. Others test fishing skills, such as casting accuracy. Competitors cast their lines and try to hit a target from a specified distance.

This competitor has caught a fine fish. He may win a prize at the fishing derby!

The big one

The biggest fishing derby in North America is the Kids All-American Fishing Derby. This derby was first held in 1987. Since then, more than eight million kids have participated in the derby! Each year, the Kids All-American Fishing Derby sponsors nearly 2,000 derbies in towns and cities across the United States. Most are free, half-day events for kids up to the age of fifteen. They usually include a cookout and other fun activities for the whole family.

Fishing etiquette

Competitors must not only follow the rules of the derby, but they must also show good fishing **etiquette**, or manners. Never deliberately frighten the fish near another angler. Give others plenty of space in which to fish, and avoid creating a shadow over their fishing areas. Don't steer your boat too close to a shore or dock where others are fishing. Step out of the water when you leave one fishing area and walk on land to get to a new spot. Respecting others shows good sportsmanship and helps ensure that there will be plenty of fish for everyone.

Fair fishing

There are several laws that anglers must obey. The laws protect fish and their **habitats**, or the natural places where fish live. Laws also ensure that all anglers will be able to enjoy fishing for many generations to come.

License to fish

Before you set out on your first fishing trip, you need to get a **fishing license**, or permission form to fish. You must buy your license from the government, and you must renew it each year. Official departments, such as the U.S. Fish and Wildlife Service, track fishing licenses to keep records of the numbers, sizes, and types of fish that are caught. Children under the age of sixteen are often allowed to fish without licenses, but the adults fishing with children must buy licenses. Make sure you check the rules in the areas where you'll be fishing and follow them.

If you catch a fish that is under the legal limit in size, you must release it. This law gives young fish a chance to become fully grown and to have babies.

Fishing for the future

Fishing laws help protect and improve fish **populations**. A population is the total number of a species living in an area. Scientists check bodies of water regularly to make sure the fish populations are large enough and that the fish are healthy. If they are not, limits may be placed on the number of each species of fish that anglers can catch. Limits are also placed during times of the year when fish **spawn**, or make babies. Allowing the fish to reproduce ensures that there will be fish to catch in the future.

Part of the ecosystem

Fish provide the world with more than food and sport. In their habitats, they eat plants and other fish. They are also food for larger fish and other animals. The pattern of eating and being eaten is called a **food chain**. When we protect fish, we help protect the entire **ecosystem**.

One of the best ways to help fish is to keep our streams, rivers, ponds, lakes, and oceans clean. The boys in the picture are picking up litter near a pond.

Signs like these help protect fish populations. Anglers should always respect the limits that are posted.

KEEPER WALLEYE MUST BE 18 INCHES RETURN ALL OTHERS

BLUEGILL
CREEL LIMIT
10 FISH DAILY
MINIMUM LENGTH
8 INCHES

Staying safe

Safety is important whenever you are in or near water. Always fish with an adult—never fish alone! To avoid rough water, check the weather before heading out on a boat and ask local anglers or guides about safe places to fish. Be sure to avoid slippery rocks and steep shores and take a careful look around before you begin fishing.

These anglers are checking the area before they begin fishing.

Don't rock the boat!

When fishing from a boat, always bring an experienced boat operator with you. Never stand up in a small motorboat or canoe, which can tip easily. Be sure to respect swimmers and other boaters. Review this safety checklist before pushing off from shore.

• Are you wearing a life jacket or personal flotation device?

• Do you have all your safety supplies? (See next page.)

• Have you told someone on land where you are going and when you'll be back?

• Has someone in the boat taken a lifesaving course?

• Did you check the weather report?

Safety supplies

Before you head out on a fishing adventure, use this checklist to ensure that you have all your safety supplies.

- Life jacket or personal flotation device
- First-aid kit, including bandages
- Sun protection, such as sunscreen, a hat, sunglasses, and a long-sleeved shirt
- Insect repellent
- Ropes, poles, or a landing net for reaching someone in the water
- Flashlight
- Torch or **flare**, if fishing from a boat
- Cellular phone or shortwave radio
- Maps
- Food and water

*The angler, shown above, is applying an **adhesive**, or sticky, bandage to a minor cut.*

The angler, shown left, is applying sunscreen to protect his skin.

Fishing for information

You can learn more about this sport by fishing around the Internet. Tackle these fun fishing websites!
www.kids-fishing.com
www.fishingforkids.net
www.ncfisheries.net/kids

Glossary

Note: Boldfaced words that are defined in the text may not appear in the glossary.

bearing The direction or position of something, relative to the position of "North" on a compass

ceramic Made of baked clay

coastal Describing the land near or along a sea or an ocean

dissolve To break down from a solid state and become part of a liquid

dorsal fin The large fin on a fish's back

ecosystem A community of living things that are connected to one another and to their surroundings

flare A device that produces a bright flame and can be used to signal that help is needed

jetty A wall or platform that is built out into a body of water and at which boats can dock

lead A heavy, soft, gray metal

oxygen A gas present in air and water that animals need to breathe

prey Animals that are hunted and eaten by other animals

spool An item shaped like a cylinder around which fishing line is wrapped

stock A supply of fish

Index

1 2 3 4 5 6 7 8 9 0 Printed in the U.S.A. 4 3 2 1 0 9 8 7 6 5